YOUR MONEY,
YOUR FUTURE

Your Money, Your Future

Investing for growth, freedom, and peace of mind in a changing environment

Michael A. Yoshikami, CFP®

Walnut Creek, CA

Your Money, Your Future
Investing for growth, freedom, and peace of mind in a changing environment
Michael A. Yoshikami, CFP*
DWM Publishing

Published by DWM Publishing, Walnut Creek, CA 94597
Copyright © 2016 by Michael A. Yoshikami, CFP*
All rights reserved.

DWM Publishing
1255 Treat Blvd., Suite 900
Walnut Creek, CA 94597
Ph +1 (925) 935-2900
E-mail: info@destinationwm.com

Publishing Manager: Helen Chang, www.authorbridgemedia.com
Editor: Kristine Serio, www.authorbridgemedia.com
Cover and Interior design: VMC Art & Design, www.vmc-artdesign.com

Library of Congress Control Number: 2015950412
ISBN: 978-0-9962916-2-0 - Softcover
      978-0-9962916-1-3 - Hardcover
      978-0-9962916-0-6 - Ebook

Ordering Information:
Quantity sales. Special discounts are available on quantity purchases by corporations, associations, and others. For details, contact the publisher at the address above.
Printed in the United States of America

ACKNOWLEDGMENTS

Thank you to our clients and business partners. We are grateful for their friendship and support.

Special thanks to my dear family and to the entire team at Destination Wealth Management, particularly those who have helped in moving this book forward to fruition. I am grateful.

CONTENTS

Introduction 9

Chapter 1 The Real Purpose of Your Money 15

Chapter 2 Identify Your Goals 24

Chapter 3 Risk versus Expectations 32

Chapter 4 Identify Investments 39

Chapter 5 Understand All the Costs before
You Invest 49

Chapter 6 Track Your Investments 56

Chapter 7 Adjust Your Portfolio to Fit
the Changing Environment 62

Chapter 8 Consider Working with an Advisor
to Maximize Your Wealth 69

Chapter 9 Enjoy Your Money 76

About the Author 81

INTRODUCTION

The Deafening Noise

You are ready to build your investment portfolio, safely and profitably. However, that is turning out to be more difficult than you thought.

Even though a tremendous amount of investing information is out there, you're having trouble distilling it. Everything you hear from the media, family, and friends should be useful, but instead it blurs together into an overwhelming challenge.

You are confused about your portfolio. Worse, the changing investing environment never stays still long enough for it to make sense. You keep making the wrong decisions and walking down paths that are not in your best interest.

Sometimes you lie awake at night, struggling to make sense of the hard questions flooding your mind: *How should I invest? What should I invest in? What's a safe investment? What's too risky?*

In the meantime, your goals and dreams are on hold. You want to retire, leave a legacy for the people you love, and create the future that you've always wanted. Without a well-thought-out investment portfolio in place, those hopes seem out of reach.

You know that investing your money profitably is possible. The choices are many, the noise around you is deafening, and you just can't see the way forward. You need a sense of clarity about the purpose and direction of your money.

You need an investment strategy that's designed specifically for you—and you need it now.

Know Yourself

The single biggest stumbling block that you face with investing is not that you don't understand the investments. It's that you don't understand yourself.

Most people haven't clearly defined what they're trying to accomplish from a financial perspective, and that has a much bigger impact on their success as investors than they realize. When you do not know exactly where you want to go, you tend to make incorrect judgments about your investments. The greater number of poor judgments you make, the more your portfolio suffers—and the further away you drift from your goals.

This concept sounds simple, but it's true. The purpose of money is not just to accumulate funds for the sake of it. Rather, money is meant to provide you with the lifestyle you hope to live in your later years. However, in order for it to work that way, you need to have a clear understanding of what you want and of what kind of person you are as an investor.

How you really think about money may not match your original assumptions. If you're figuring out an investment strategy with a partner, you may be surprised to discover the ways in which the other person's views differ from yours.

Too often, people invest based on what others think is important. That is simply the wrong way to approach investing. You have to invest based on what *you* think is important. When you learn to invest based on your personal values and goals, the investing paradigm of frustration and confusion can shift to one of success.

My Mission

My understanding of investing isn't theoretical. It comes from decades of practical knowledge and experience.

I've been helping people invest for more than thirty years. I am the Founder and CEO of Destination Wealth Management (DWM), a financial planning and investment firm that tailors investment solutions to meet the needs of clients from all walks of life. I come from humble beginnings, having started my company in my twenties, and I worked hard to build DWM into a firm that truly helps others.

I wasn't a rich kid. I worked my way through college, and I know the value of a dollar. I also know the value of being prudent with financial resources. Investing is not a game. Rather, it is a serious business of making sure that your investment strategies match your life goals.

My family is originally from Hawaii, where "aloha" is something real and tangible, and I've always focused on helping others as best as I could. That sense of responsibility to give back is what drew me to the investment business more than thirty-five years ago. It continues to drive me today.

My mission, and the mission of my company, is to make a positive difference in clients' lives. I see firsthand how our efforts to improve their futures pay off every day. Our entire staff is dedicated to that purpose.

This book is an extension of that mission. I truly believe that the concepts in these chapters will make a positive difference for you, just as they do for our clients.

Build Your Compass

This book is not an academic thesis. It is a practical guide designed to help you build a personal compass that will lead you to an investment strategy that is right for you.

Digest the concepts in these chapters over time. Use the pages as a workbook, and make notes on the things that are important to you based on what you're trying to achieve. Ask your investment advisor questions straight out of your notes. Once you've read the whole book, stand back for a moment and see if you can come up with an overall philosophy on how you think you should be investing, based on who you are.

There are thousands of books out there on all the different types of investment possibilities available. This book is not one of them. Instead, it is designed to be the key that unlocks all of those other doors. It combines goal clarification with behavioral analysis. It is meant to give you the foundation to make the right decisions for your unique objectives.

Your investment opportunities and circumstances may change over time. But as long as you build the right personal compass using the strategies in these chapters, you will know how to proceed on your investing journey.

This book will be your guide. From there, it is up to you to walk the path toward personal financial success.

Navigate Your Investments

Too often, investors talk about their money in a way that is completely disconnected from how they really live their lives. They envision opulent lifestyles for themselves, but without making the decisions today that are necessary to live that future life. They scrimp and save on a daily basis, depriving themselves of a comfortable lifestyle now even though they have no intention of spending large sums of money in the future. This doesn't have to be your story.

The expression "to thine own self be true" is certainly accurate, and never is it more important than when you are making decisions as an investor. We are talking about more than just your money. We are talking about your future.

By the time you turn the last page of this book, you will have a framework that you can use to make sound judgments about how to invest for growth, freedom, and peace of mind in a changing environment, both now and in later years—a framework that is tailor-made for you and your goals.

You will have the compass you need to navigate today's challenging investment environment.

Chapter 1

THE REAL PURPOSE
OF YOUR MONEY

A Fresh Start

Ines and Mark came to my office to discuss their portfolio. Outside, it was a bright spring morning. Conversely, their faces were full of shadows, fearful and concerned.

They had tried to invest before. However, everything had gone wrong.

The advice they received on their investments had caused them to end up with a high-risk strategy—and they had absolutely no idea that this was the case. Their portfolio had been stagnant for years. No one had adjusted it to match what was happening in the environment. When the economic crash of 2008 occurred, they lost 50 percent of their portfolio . . . and they had not forgotten that pain.

This bad experience traumatized the couple even more than it would have affected the average person. Ines and Mark were conservative people in their mid-sixties who had been married for forty years. Their parents had experienced the Great Depression, and Ines and Mark had worked hard to build up a portfolio. Their first jobs had been in agriculture, working in a factory for less than fifty cents an hour. They knew the value of money.

The couple hoped to provide college funds for their two grandchildren, but apart from that, their goals were simple. They did not live an extravagant lifestyle. They just wanted to be comfortable and live out the rest of their lives without anxiety and concern, enjoying the fruits of their labor from the many years that they had worked.

That day in my office, I helped Ines and Mark make a fresh start with their investments. I listened carefully to their values and designed a new plan to fit their personal risk-return profile. I explained the new strategy clearly with custom charts and encouraged them to ask questions. I also put in place a plan to track and adjust their portfolio in the coming years, so that they could rest easy about the future.

Ines and Mark walked out of my office that day tremendously relieved. No longer did they have to wonder what their strategy was to achieve their goals, or invest in the dark without a compass, worried that it was too late to find success.

After years of uncertainty, they were finally on a path they understood.

The Real Purpose of Your Money

The world is changing rapidly.

You only need to pick up the newspaper, turn on the TV, or browse the Web to see it. Life is moving faster. World economies are becoming more closely aligned. People are living longer. All of that taken together makes investment decisions more complicated than they've ever been.

Some investors try to ignore this. They put their heads in the sand and hope that, above ground, everything will magically work out.

Putting your head in the sand might have been a reasonable strategy in the past. Now it is a recipe for disaster. You need to understand what's going on around you. More importantly, you need to understand who you are, where you stand, and what your goals are in order to invest well.

You need to understand the real purpose of your money.

Your money is not a Monopoly game. Rather, it is a tool that can be used to meet financial challenges and retirement goals.

That is why it is so important to understand what you are trying to accomplish with your money before you start investing. You have goals to live a certain lifestyle, and perhaps to leave a legacy for the people and organizations closest to you. Those things can only be achieved if you put together a strategy that fits your comfort level and is designed for your unique goals.

Not every investment is a "one-size-fits-all"

proposition. That's why you can't just read a book about how to invest in a specific asset and expect it to work for you. There are investments that will fit your personal needs and move you closer to your goals, and there are investments that could derail your strategy altogether.

Think of it like this: if you are a family of eight, you need to buy a van—not a two-seat sports car—to get you where you need to go. The investment vehicle you choose works the same way. You need the right vehicle for what you are trying to accomplish. When you gain a basic understanding of what is important to you and what kinds of risk you're comfortable with, you empower yourself to choose a strategy that fits you.

You cannot close your eyes and expect to achieve your investing goals in a financial landscape that changes this rapidly. You need to sharpen your awareness of two things: your personal values as an investor and your understanding of the new investing environment.

The New Investing Environment

As I mentioned earlier, the new investing environment is driven by constant change.

Technology has transformed the way information is distributed. That distribution is more democratized than ever. Information has become a vastly available commodity, and anyone has the power to act immediately on what he or she hears.

In other words, all of us now have the ability to panic in real time, and that creates incredible volatility. Combined with technology that allows for bursts of trading, fluctuation is now the norm.

The new investing environment means that there is more opportunity to be wrong in a magnified way. The cost of an investment mistake has never been higher, and the world is littered with investors who have not thought carefully about their financial strategies and, as a result, suffered irreparable long-term harm.

Globalization is also becoming a bigger issue, as economies become more closely linked, thanks to monetary agencies and trade agreements. This isn't a passing fad. It's a permanent condition, and it will only accelerate as trade borders continue to crumble and global business transactions become easier.

All of this means one thing for you, as an investor: you need to learn to adapt.

This doesn't mean throwing away the old investment adages that have served you well in years past. Nothing could be further from the truth. What it means is that you need to integrate those old philosophies with the new environment and make changes accordingly.

However, while the environment plays a key role, it's not the whole story. You can't make changes until you know who you are as an investor. You can't adapt until you've clarified what kind of risk you're comfortable with, what your values are, and what goals you envision for your future. Before you know these things, your attempts at adaptation will be hollow, because you'll just be going through motions that someone else has laid out for you—motions that don't have anything to do with what matters to you as an individual.

That's where the rest of this book comes in.

The Investor's Compass

In the chapters that follow, I will walk you through the process of understanding yourself as an investor, and then using that understanding to make decisions that are right for you in a volatile investing environment.

Building your personal investing compass is an eight-step process. The following chapters have each been organized around each of these steps.

Identify your goals.

A significant part of understanding who you are as an investor is identifying your goals. Going through this identification process will help you determine what you are trying to achieve with your money. It doesn't matter what other people's goals are. What matters is what is important to you.

Identify your level of risk.

Your level of risk and your return expectations are directly connected to what you're trying to achieve.

Analyzing risk puts you in a position to see whether your strategy is appropriate.

Identify investments that fit your risk-expectation profile.
After you've identified what you're trying to achieve and the risk you are willing to take to achieve it, the next step is to identify the types of investments that will fit best with your strategy.

Understand all the costs before you invest.
Understanding all the costs of an investment may sound simple, but it can be much more complex than many people realize. Beyond the investments themselves, you need to know if the people you're working with are making commissions or receiving other compensation that might affect their objective assessment of your portfolio strategy. You need to know all costs before you invest.

Track your investments.
It's important to not only make the right investments, but also keep track of how things are going after you have invested. This is true even if you delegate the responsibility of making the investments to an investment manager. The more informed you are about how your investments are doing, the better chance you'll have of accomplishing your goals.

Adjust your portfolio to fit the changing environment.
In today's environment, you must adapt and adjust

your investment strategy as time goes on. This is true whether you are investing for the short or long term. As conditions change, you must be tactical about your investing decisions if you hope to achieve success.

Consider professional assistance.
This is important if you have neither the time nor inclination to invest your portfolio yourself. In the right situations, working with an advisor can be an important part of financial success. Advisors can give you feedback on how reasonable your goals are and help you create a roadmap for how to achieve them. You need an advisor who is competent, transparent, and easy to communicate with so that you can fully take advantage of the services provided.

Enjoy your money.
There is no point in scrimping and saving all your life if you're not going to take advantage of your hard work in later years. Your savings are intended to provide you with comfort and joy in your later years. As long as your investment strategy is consistent with what you're trying to achieve, there is no reason you should not be able to truly enjoy your money and the lifestyle it provides.

These eight steps taken together will allow you to create a custom-built compass to help you make effective decisions as an investor. Embracing these concepts will allow you to get where you want to go financially and avoid the mistakes that most investors make along the way.

In the end, your goal as an investor should be to know yourself so that you can achieve the goals you're aiming for with your investment strategy. The process I'm about to guide you through will give you a framework for doing exactly that.

By the time you finish this book, you will understand how to invest in a way that feels comfortable for you. You'll be able to sleep at night, knowing that your money is working on your behalf to move you in the direction of the future you want.

Never allow others to tell you what is important to you, or dictate who you are as an investor. You are fully capable of deciding what's important for yourself and setting objectives that support those values. The first step in accomplishing that is identifying your goals.

Chapter 2

IDENTIFY YOUR GOALS

A Question of Goals

I recently gave a talk at an event in San Francisco, California, on the alarming fluctuations of equity markets. At the end of the talk, I asked if there were any questions.

One woman in the audience raised her hand and stood up. "My husband and I are in our fifties, and we want to make as much money as possible. How should we do it?" she asked.

I looked at her for a moment. She and the rest of the audience were clearly expecting me to give a simple answer that would solve every one of their investment problems.

I considered my words carefully before I responded. This type of question required a delicate answer.

"Well, wanting to make money is an obvious goal of every investor," I said. "But your investment strategy can't be based on just making as much money as possible. You need to determine what you are trying to accomplish on a tangible, objective basis."

Then, right there on stage, I walked the woman through a verbal questionnaire about her and her husband's goals: What lifestyle did they aspire to have when they both retired? Did they still want to continue working after retirement? What was their personal definition of financial happiness? How much risk could they endure?

By the end of the discussion, the woman had a different view of her question.

"Maybe we're not just looking to make a lot of money," she admitted. "Maybe we're actually looking to retire comfortably in ten years."

She and everyone else in the audience had a moment of awareness about how investment goals work. They realized that those unique goals were at the heart of what was needed to drive their investment strategies. Instead of being so focused on making as much money as possible, they finally got down to the real issue: retiring comfortably.

Making as much money as possible is a great idea, and I am certainly not opposed to that. However, that effort should be synchronized with real and tangible objectives.

Shoot for Your Goal

What are goals, in the context of investing?

A goal is what you define to be the purpose of your investments. For this reason, goals are the foundation of any investment strategy. They are part of the map that shows you how to use your money to create the future you want. In order to understand how you wish to invest, you must first understand what you're trying to accomplish based on your personal value system and what is important to you.

This is a critical part of building your personal compass as an investor. Once you define your goals, you understand that money is the main driver to help you achieve the lifestyle you want—and that awareness alone makes you far better off than most investors.

Goals are never vague things. The media continually suggests that every investor's goal should simply be to get rich quick, without any real recognition of what that money is meant to accomplish. This short-term reactionary perspective has no place in a prudent, thoughtful investment portfolio strategy.

What you need are goals comprising concrete numbers that align with the specific lifestyle you envision for yourself in the future. These numbers will become your standards of measurement, allowing you to determine whether you're on the path to success.

Maybe the thing most important to you is simply financial security. Or maybe you have something even more tangible in mind, such as a retirement property, living comfortably without relying on your children, relocating to another part of the world upon your retirement, or traveling.

Regardless, identifying goals is about explicitly answering this question: What is the long-term purpose of your money? Is it for you, others, or both? Is it designed to leave a legacy for charities that are important to you? Are your main goals about security, lifestyle, or some combination of these two things?

The answers to these questions vary greatly from person to person. The important things to consider are the questions themselves, and whether you have honestly asked yourself every one of them. In this chapter, I'll walk you through the questions I ask my clients about their goals, so that you can identify your own personal key queries for making your investments.

How to Identify Your Goals

Your goals evolve naturally as the years go on. However, regardless of what stage of life you find yourself in, you need to be clear about the short- and long-term goals you have for your investments. This is true whether you are investing as an individual or as a couple.

How do you go about identifying investing goals?

For most individuals, goal identification is a matter of simply sitting down and being honest about your dreams and priorities. Ask yourself the following four questions to begin the process of outlining clear short- and long-term goals for your money:

What does money mean to you?
Before you can set specific goals, you need to have a

clear understanding of what money means to you. Your views on money will dictate your goals.

Ask yourself: What does being financially secure mean to me? Be very clear on this point before you move on.

What does a successful retirement look like?

Once you understand your personal attitude toward money, the next thing to consider is what a secure retirement means to you. Again, a good grasp of this concept will be key to setting strong goals. If retirement is your destination, you should design your goals to provide the kind of retirement you want.

Ask yourself: What lifestyle do I envision for myself in retirement? How much money do I need to do the things I want to do when I retire? Make sure to consider enjoyment as well as comfort and security when you pose these questions to yourself.

What are your long-term financial goals?

After you have identified what retirement means to you, get more specific about your long-term financial goals. Take your general ideas about your ideal retirement and make them quantifiable.

For example, perhaps your ideal retirement means traveling around the world. To make that more specific, you might ask yourself how many trips you want to take. Do you want to go abroad every three months? Twice per year? What is the average cost of a trip based on your personal travel standards? How much money do you want to have per month to make this happen during your retirement?

When considering your long-term financial goals, you should also consider when you plan to retire. Your long-term goals will obviously be different if you plan to retire in five years as opposed to twenty years. Be sure to take the timeline into account.

What are your short-term financial goals?

Last but not least, you need to factor the present into your investing goals, along with the future. Your understanding of your long-term goals will affect your decisions on more immediate short-term goals.

Ask yourself: What do I want in the short term? Do I want to buy a new home? Build up college savings? Create an emergency fund? Go on a dream vacation?

With a clear picture of what you want to achieve, you have a key part of the frame of reference you need to make the best possible investing decisions with your money. However, those decisions may not be up to you alone. You may need to factor in another consideration: your significant other.

Shared Goals

When identifying your investment goals with a significant other, there are additional factors to consider.

Couples are often surprised by how much their views differ when it comes to investing.

For example, two clients of mine (a couple) came from very different financial backgrounds. The husband's mother had grown up in a very fiscally restrained family, and he was influenced by her view that protecting principal was the most important priority in any investment plan.

Meanwhile, the wife was the daughter of a technology company executive. She had seen the rise and fall of several technology companies, and she felt that volatility was a natural part of investing; she was comfortable with fluctuation.

Their views on risk were polar opposites, and finding a middle ground for their portfolio was a challenge that took some time to figure out.

You and your significant other may hold different views of money for any number of reasons. Regardless of why you believe what you believe, you need to consider your partner's values when you set investing goals.

To do this, it is important to recognize that couples may have fundamentally different goals in life. Because of this, it is necessary to recognize each individual's goals before coming together to find the common ground.

A good way to begin is for each of you to prioritize your own personal goals in order of importance. Then, together, determine how important each goal is for you as a couple. If you and your spouse have very different views on money, it then becomes especially important to focus on the end goal of what you hope to accomplish with your money, rather than on the money itself.

Aim for Something

The famous Zig Ziglar quote says it best: "If you aim at nothing, you will hit it every time."

Problems occur as an investor if you aim at a target that someone else sets for you instead of identifying goals based on your personal values. Many investors listen to what the financial experts are saying in the media, but they don't really analyze whether the advice is specifically right for them. This is a big mistake that can have significant negative consequences on their portfolios.

In my years as an advisor, I have seen a wide spectrum of investors. Many have succeeded; many others have failed. Invariably, the ones who succeed are the ones who clearly define goals for their money before they start investing. They've reduced the confusion of the investing process by identifying exactly where they want to go.

Fortunately, they don't stop there.

Once they have their goals, they take things a step further. They develop an investment strategy that will move them toward their specific objectives. That strategy starts with the basics: identifying the level of risk they're comfortable with and the amount of return expected in exchange for that risk. I'll walk you through the process of how to do this in the next chapter.

Chapter 3

RISK VERSUS EXPECTATIONS

A Risky Ride

John and Elisa had been through investment disaster twice before.

The first time was in 2001, when they were invested heavily in Internet stocks. Many of their friends worked in Silicon Valley. "Brick-and-mortar-type businesses are dying out," those friends said. "The future of the world has everything to do with the Internet." Despite warnings from other people that the risk of investing in emerging technology was high, John and Elisa had faith in this prediction. They were believers, and they moved their whole portfolio toward this new strategy.

Then the dot-com stock-market crash happened— taking with it two-thirds of the money that they had worked a lifetime to accumulate.

John and Elisa decided that they would never again fall victim to that kind of debacle. From now on, they would invest in something that could not possibly lose: real estate. Owning tangible properties was different from owning stocks, they reasoned. They could borrow money cheaply and rent out the houses, all while experiencing value appreciation of 20 percent per year. Real estate would help them recover from the dot-com fiasco.

Then *that* bubble popped. They couldn't believe it when the housing market crashed in 2007. Once again they were faced with unthinkable losses.

After the second disaster, John and Elisa realized that they had not understood clearly the risks that came along with their investments. They felt that there must be a way to invest successfully, but they certainly hadn't found it.

"What is the secret?" they wondered.

Types of Risk

Like John and Elisa, before you can invest successfully, you need to fully understand the risk and reward factors of your investment plan.

"Risk" can mean different things to different people. Most investors are familiar with fluctuation risk, in which the value of an asset rises or falls. However, fluctuation risk is far from the only type of risk you need to take into account when investing.

For example, you may need to consider interest-rate risk—the negative fluctuation of bond assets when interest rates rise. There is also purchasing-power risk—the risk of losing purchasing power as inflation rises over time. Liquidity risk means that assets cannot be easily liquidated and turned into cash, something that often occurs in real estate investments, limited partnerships, and types of bonds. Last but not least, default risk refers to what you stand to lose if a company or organization defaults on an interest payment.

Before you invest, you need to carefully assess each different type of risk. Understanding how much risk you can tolerate matters a great deal when you are looking at investment opportunities.

Investors have a tendency to make the worst possible decisions at the worst possible times—namely, when volatility rears its ugly head and they aren't expecting it. Understanding risk before it arises is critical if one is to avoid rash reactions.

You can't wait to identify the level of risk you're willing to endure until that risk is knocking on the front door. At that point, it's too late, and you're faced with unpleasant choices that are often wrapped in a considerable dose of emotion.

Remember, your retirement assets are not like dealing with discretionary income or assets. You need this money to support your long-term plans for your future. That is why you need to identify from the start the level of risk you're comfortable with, as well as what you expect to get in exchange for it.

You should seek to design a portfolio strategy that

delivers a risk level you are comfortable with, combined with an acceptable return expectation. In this chapter, I will show you how to identify your personal level of risk and adjust your expectations accordingly.

Identify Your Level of Risk Tolerance

How do you identify your risk comfort level?

This process can be complicated, as you will have to balance short- and long-term goals. If the risk you're trying to figure out is related to fluctuation, then when identifying your level of risk tolerance, you need to ask yourself: How much fluctuation can I endure before I start making decisions that will have a negative impact on my long-term strategy? At what point might I abandon my strategy altogether?

It's important that every investor recognizes what his or her downside comfort level is. Of course, it is also important to balance downside protection with upside appreciation, and that balance must be assessed carefully.

Take the time to actually imagine how you will feel when a worst-case scenario happens. This visualization will help you determine whether you can really stomach the potential value downdraft. It's the most straightforward path to determining the magnitude of fluctuation you can honestly live with.

Beyond the numbers, however, there's another form

of risk you need to take into account during this process: the risk of not reaching your goals.

Investors are sometimes so afraid of taking any risk at all in their portfolio strategy that they end up leaving considerable returns on the table. This is especially true of portfolios with longer timelines.

For example, if you have twenty years ahead of you before you're ready to put your investment money to use in your retirement, you can probably live with some degree of fluctuation along the way, as long as you keep that long-term horizon in mind. Not taking on enough risk to meet your goals can be just as negative as taking on more risk than you're comfortable with.

Return Expectations versus Risk

Risk is directly related to the potential for return. Never believe anyone who tells you that low risk and high return is a reasonable outcome; it is simply not the case.

Awareness of your risk-tolerance level allows you to make a judgment call as to how much fluctuation you are comfortable enduring related to the return you are hoping to achieve. Obviously, this balancing act requires careful consideration, since investment choices are all about tradeoffs relative to return and risk.

Meticulous research on past performance and future return expectations relative to fluctuation levels can give you an idea of the type of returns you might expect for the risk you are taking. Carefully consider your emotional reaction when bad news pops up and causes a fluctuation in an asset or strategy. As stated previously, the last thing you want to do is react impulsively at the worst possible moment when negative fluctuation occurs.

The decision you must make is clear: How much fluctuation are you willing to tolerate relative to the return you hope to receive?

Take Action

After identifying your level of risk tolerance, you might look at your portfolio and find that it includes much more risk than you are comfortable with. Then you need to carefully examine exactly how you're invested and find places where you can make adjustments that will reduce your risk. If you are working with an advisor, that individual can put your portfolio through a stress test for you, so that you know exactly what embedded potential fluctuation is in your portfolio.

You need to be fearless and objective when you go through this process. Adjusting your portfolio to match your risk comfort level can be challenging. Sometimes it can mean selling assets that you've liked in the past, or selling assets at a loss. Sometimes it means parting ways with strategies that you are invested in, not just in terms of money, but on emotional and intellectual grounds as well.

The bottom line is that if your overall portfolio does not match your current risk-tolerance level, you're going to have problems with your strategy when bad news comes along. Review your strategy carefully, come up with an honest assessment of its risks and rewards, and adjust it as necessary to make sure it will work for you in the long term.

Risk and Reward

When you identify your risk level and expectations up front, you empower yourself to make good choices before you invest, rather than putting yourself in a position of reacting to fluctuation at the worst possible moment. This reduces the chance of potential outcomes being beyond your understanding or expectation.

Understanding your risk-expectation profile is one of the most important steps for you to take as you develop your investment plan. Once you have clarity on this important concept, you're ready to start using your investing compass to identify investments that are right for you.

Chapter 4

IDENTIFY INVESTMENTS

Diversification Delusion

"I'm a believer in diversification, and I already have a diverse portfolio. I've bought different assets, and I think I have a great mix of them. I just want you to double-check my portfolio."

That was what Daryl said when he walked into my office. There wasn't an ounce of doubt in his voice. He felt very confident about his strategy.

I read his portfolio statement and made a quick assessment. His assets certainly looked diverse on the surface; there were plenty of names. But right away, I saw a problem.

"All of your stocks are very similar in terms of industry," I told Daryl. "You own seven stocks in tele-communications, six in technology, and a variety of others in financial services." I looked him in the eye. "They all appear to be different. But your portfolio isn't really diversified."

I described for him what a truly diversified asset base looks like, and we discussed the concept of non-correlation. Then we talked for a while about portfolio construction.

Up until then, Daryl thought all was well, believing his portfolio to be a diversified mix of assets that reflected his self-described conservative risk appetite. As we talked though, Daryl slowly started to realize that what he had developed was only a start, rather than the truly diversified allocation he had hoped to construct. When he understood what was really going on, he nervously asked me, "What do I do now?"

Together, we went through the identification of goals exercise, followed by an evaluation of his risk profile. After clarifying these points, we put together a portfolio that was significantly more diversified, utilizing many types of assets.

After our meeting, Daryl felt more comfortable and in control. He was able to adjust his portfolio and significantly increase its diversification. His new plan was not so subject to the whim of assets that would likely all move at the same time in the same direction. That was exactly where he wanted to be.

Investment ID

With your personal risk profile in hand, you're ready to begin identifying investments that are a good fit for your portfolio. The key to this step of investing is diversification.

Diversification simply means not having all your eggs in one basket. It is one of the most effective ways to minimize your amount of risk when you invest. As such, it is a prudent step regardless of whether you're comfortable with a high level of risk. Diversification reduces the amount of concentration in your portfolio, and that can help you in developing a plan designed to provide the most optimal chance of achieving your goals.

Diversifying your portfolio is more important now than ever before. As I mentioned in the first chapter, we live in a highly connected and rapidly changing world. Because of this, investors can react simultaneously to new information, and this leads to huge fluctuations in the market. Volatility is a permanent feature of the new investing environment. Markets around the world are more correlated than ever, and fear or euphoria spreads globally in contagion fashion.

For instance, if I told you that the US stock market went down 3 percent today, what direction would you assume the European or Chinese stock market would go tomorrow? You would probably expect that they would also go down—and you would likely be right.

Markets, interest rate policies, and economic decisions are now interlinked so tightly that you are likely to see an impact on your portfolio no matter where change is happening in the world. That is why diversification is so important.

Even when you try to diversify, however, portfolio assets can still be closely correlated. This means that they tend to move together in similar ways. While you might enjoy the idea of all your assets going up at the same time, a non-diversified portfolio strategy means that they can all go down at the same time as well.

The key to true, effective diversification is understanding the movement between held assets. This is about more than just investing in a number of different names in your portfolio. It means that you should consider diversification across different sectors: international versus domestic, small versus large, dividend versus non-dividend, value versus growth, and so forth.

It's important to note that this chapter in the book is not designed to cover the details of each investment asset. That process requires careful analysis and, in many cases, professional assistance. However, this chapter will give you a broad overview of the different types of securities that may be appropriate for your investment strategy.

Types of Assets

Scores of books focus on the types of investments available to investors. A quick Internet search shows millions of resources extolling the virtues of certain assets or Web opinions.

Rather than attempting to go into the many nuances of specific investment vehicles here, this chapter will provide a simple outline of the types of assets most investors utilize when considering an investment plan. It is not exhaustive or detailed; again, that is by design. This summary is focused on providing a basic framework for further investigation as you develop your strategy. It is the starting point for your investment design process.

The asset types covered below exclude certain categories of investment alternatives, such as private equity funds, hedge assets, direct real estate ownership, collectibles, and other less-commonly held investment vehicles. Despite their exclusion from this summary, these assets may be appropriate for you and may merit additional investigation as you develop your investment plan.

You can invest in a number of different types of assets. The most common categories include equity positions, fixed income and preferred stock, commodities, real estate investment trusts, and cash.

Equity Positions
The three main types of equity positions are individual stocks, mutual funds, and exchange traded fund assets (ETFs).

Individual equity positions are direct investments in a company's shares. These assets can be either domestic or international. Some of them are highly liquid, while others have limited liquidity, meaning that shares are not as easily traded—something that can impact the price when you move to buy or sell that security. Individual equity positions can be growth stocks or value stocks.

Individual stocks may or may not pay dividends on an ongoing basis. Stocks vary by sector, capitalization size, and other factors.

Equity mutual funds can be classified as value or growth, large or small, and dividend paying or non-dividend paying, as well as a host of other classifications. They can also be scored by rating agencies such as Value Line and Morningstar to assess their performances relative to their peers. Funds have a manager and charge an internal fee for this oversight. Equity mutual funds tend to be diversified in the number of names they hold, but may not be diversified in other respects; it depends on the fund. Some funds hold as few as thirty or forty positions, while others own hundreds of positions. Index funds are also a form of funds that have gained popularity in recent years (popular in that they are low cost and not managed). You need to be clear on the details of each fund when you build them into your overall portfolio strategy.

ETFs are an increasingly popular investment instrument. They are similar to index assets, but are traded as stocks. For the most part, ETFs are non-managed entities, though new investment classes called "actively managed ETF assets" are emerging. The variables of ETFs are the same as they are for stocks and mutual funds. With ETFs, the important thing to keep in mind is that they do not usually have active managers like mutual fund companies. However, the advantage of these assets is that they are low cost and often targeted in terms of the focus area.

Fixed-Income Assets and Preferred Stocks

"Fixed income" is generally a synonymous term for bonds. With bonds, you agree to invest with a company, they agree to repay you within a set period, and as an exchange they provide interest along the way. The risk-versus-return characteristics of bonds are often impacted by the credit quality of the company issuing the bond and the length of maturity of the bonds themselves.

Preferred stocks are similar to bonds but tend to have very long maturity dates, if they mature at all. This type of asset is further down on the liquidation scale, meaning that if the company declares bankruptcy, bondholders will be paid before preferred stockholders. Preferred stocks tend to have a fluctuating price—just as fixed-income positions do—and pay dividend yields.

The types of fixed income and preferred stock you invest in can vary greatly. Variables you need to assess include maturity dates, credit quality, date of origination, sector risk, and other items. Although fixed income and preferred stocks experience fluctuation, it is usually lower than the fluctuation that can occur with equity positions. Fixed-income and preferred stock positions are usually included in a portfolio designed to provide an income stream.

Commodities

Commodities are tangible assets. A tangible asset is just about anything you can hold in your hand: gold, lumber, paper, oil, and other hard assets.

Investors often use commodities as a hedge against inflation, since commodity prices tend to rise over the long term as inflation picks up. Commodities are impacted not only by demand and supply, but also by currency fluctuation. The overall health of the economy impacts commodity prices.

Buying commodities on a direct basis can be difficult. For this reason, most investors choose to buy commodities through ETFs and mutual funds when they decide to add them to their overall portfolio strategies.

Real Estate Investment Trusts

Real estate investment trusts allow investors to buy a small unit of a trust that invests solely in real estate, either commercial or residential. They are a way for you to buy real estate without having to get the loan or do the diligence related to each individual property yourself. The idea is that you are hiring an experienced real estate investor to make the investment on your behalf in exchange for part of the overall profit.

Real estate trusts tend to pay annual distributions. The payouts can vary greatly, and will largely depend on the risks associated with the investments in the trust. Investors sometimes buy real estate investment trusts to participate in perceived rising real estate prices as a hedge against inflation. However, the value of your investment is impacted when interest rates rise in the short term, which tends to negatively impact these trusts in rising interest rate environments.

Cash

Cash and other types of short-term obligations are designed to provide liquidity to your portfolio strategy, giving you emergency reserves.

The yield for cash and fixed-income type assets that have short maturities (anything below 270 days) tends to be low. Therefore, the goal with cash is not so much to invest for return, but rather to give your portfolio more stability. Cash is also used as a way to park your money until other investment decisions can be made.

The Best Mix for You

Having been through the different types of assets, the obvious question is: What is the best mix for you and your goals?

You can achieve some level of diversification by combining a number of the assets we've just covered in your overall portfolio strategy. However, the best mix for you will depend on a number of factors, many of which were defined in previous chapters.

Perhaps the most important among these factors is whether you can live with the fluctuations associated with a given portfolio strategy. After defining the annual return you seek based on a reasonable financial plan, you can then start designing an investment plan in order to meet your goals.

The construction of your portfolio strategy is critical

for obvious reasons; namely, it is the vehicle to move you forward toward your planning objectives. For that reason, it is important to construct your strategy in a thoughtful and transparent way. Sometimes it can be difficult to know what's in a mutual fund or an ETF asset, and it helps to take advantage of tools in order to make your assessments. A dependable advisor can be a useful ally at this stage of the process. I'll explain more about choosing and working with a good advisor in chapter 8.

All the Moving Pieces

At this stage in the process, you are beginning to see how all the moving pieces of your portfolio strategy fit together.

Never underestimate diversification. Without it, you are setting yourself up for more volatility than you might be comfortable with in your investment strategy should the wrong kind of news occur.

Identifying the moving pieces, however, does not stop with diversification. In chapter 5, I'll take you through the next step in creating a personalized portfolio strategy: understanding the costs and fees of your investments.

UNDERSTAND ALL THE COSTS BEFORE YOU INVEST

Invisible Numbers

"But I don't understand," Elena said. "I bought a supposedly no-cost variable annuity. There weren't any sales charges when I first invested in it. So what are these fees, and how are they impacting my returns?"

Elena and I met at a seminar organized by a large financial institution, where I'm a regular featured speaker. She was a smart single mom who had persevered and worked hard in the face of many challenges to reach her current level of success. Elena had come to the seminar eager to find out more about investment strategies that might be a good fit for her.

We discussed her investments, and as you can imagine, she was not happy when I told her that no upfront cost does not mean no internal fees.

High internal fees were being charged on Elena's

"no-cost" annuity. Not only was she dealing with management fees for the sub-accounts that the annuity was being invested in, she was also paying something called a mortality expense charge—a fee that provides a life insurance component in certain variable annuities.

The company Elena had invested with was required to provide her with this information on the fees and charges. However, the fees didn't show up in an easy-to-read statement, and as a result, Elena had not really digested the reality of the embedded fees.

This is a common story that all investors should understand. Investments have associated fees, and it's important to thoughtfully investigate all costs that can impact your returns.

The Real Cost of Investing

When it comes to investing, identifying costs is more complex than it seems. Your investing costs encompass far more than just what you pay for the investment itself. Things like fees and commissions factor into nearly every investment you make. Unfortunately, most people are not aware of the costs associated with their investments, and uninformed investors are paying fees they didn't even know existed.

Fees are confusing. How many investors who buy mutual funds really understand the fees associated with the ongoing management of their portfolios? How many investors work with advisors and stockbrokers without ever fully comprehending the amount they're paying those individuals in fees?

It's important to understand the costs associated with the different assets in your portfolio. Fees impact your overall return and, if you're not aware of them, that can ultimately derail the effectiveness of your overall strategy.

For example, let's say you invest in something that supposedly provides you a 10 percent return in one year. That sounds great, right? But what if you have to pay 3 percent per year in fees? That's 30 percent of the overall return on your money, and 30 percent is a big number to pay on an ongoing basis.

The impact can be even greater if you invest in fixed-income type assets. Now, instead of earning 10 percent, you are only earning 4 percent to begin with, and 3 percent of that is going toward fees. That wipes out a huge portion of your total return.

This is why investors are so understandably sensitive to paying fees—and it is also why you need to recognize exactly how much you're paying when you invest. In this chapter, I'll give you an overview of the different types of fees you may encounter when you invest.

Understand All the Costs

When I say you need to understand "all the costs" of investing, what costs am I referring to?

Simply put, I am referring to *all* the costs—not just the obvious ones!

Your costs can include investment management fees, brokerage costs, management fees from mutual fund managers and ETF providers, commissions, the margin between purchasing an asset at market value and buying it from the broker's inventory (sometimes called "spread"), insurance or mortality costs, and a variety of less-common charges. Let's take a look at each of these central categories.

Investment Management Fees

Investment management fees charged by fund companies and advisors are typically calculated based as a percentage of assets managed by the manager. For example, if a client has a $1,000,000 portfolio, the annual fees might be 1 percent, or $10,000 per year. As such, if a portfolio achieved a gross return of 10 percent for a period, or $100,000, the net return would be $90,000, or 9 percent.

Brokerage Costs

Brokerage costs are the fees your brokers charge for the services they provide to you. Brokers typically charge fees for services such as trade execution, financial planning, and investment advice.

Mutual Fund and ETF Provider Management Fees

Mutual fund and ETF provider management fees must be deducted from gross returns to arrive at net returns.

These fees are designed to pay institutional costs and ongoing expenses.

Commissions

Brokers may charge you commissions for certain trades. This may be an upfront transactional cost.

Spreads

Spreads normally represent the difference in price between the purchase price and selling price in a financial instrument. For securities, it is the difference between the bid and the asking price. Spreads can also exist, with a few differences, in stocks, bonds, commodities, options, and foreign currency, as well as a few other financial products and assets.

Insurance and Mortality Costs

Insurance costs in variable annuities and life insurance are calculated by considering several factors, which include mortality costs and operational costs (including agent commissions). For example, mortality costs, the largest component of insurance costs, are the costs of paying claims to the beneficiaries of the insured.

The Value of Fees

Fees are not inherently bad. They can cover useful and important services. As with anything else you buy, the thing to consider is whether you feel you are getting value for the fees charged.

You're going to pay fees, in one way or another, even if you self-manage everything you invest in. While self-managing is a possibility that may seem to save you money on fees in the short run, if you're not implementing your strategy perfectly from the start, it could prove to be costly in the end.

Investment companies and managers understandably expect to get paid for their expertise. There's nothing wrong with that. What matters is that you very clearly identify what fees you're paying. Make sure you assess the full list of fees when you invest, so that you have a strong grasp of the real cost structure for your portfolio.

Anyone you work with must be able to tell you what the fee structure is for the assets in your portfolio strategy. Your advisor should be comfortable disclosing the fees, including commissions, and should not be evasive or defensive about this issue. You have a right to know the fees you are paying.

Make sure the fees you're being charged are fair. However, don't sacrifice the service you need in pursuit of chasing the lowest fee available, only to find that your money has been invested incorrectly in the long run.

Full Disclosure

It makes sense for you to understand exactly how much

you are paying for the asset strategy you're investing in. Do not be shy about demanding disclosure of all the costs when you invest.

Full disclosure will allow you to make an accurate judgment about whether you're getting what you need from your investment or the professionals providing the service. Be an informed consumer who understands the impact of fees on your portfolio strategy.

You are now ready to assess the progress of your investment strategy: tracking your investments.

Chapter 6

TRACK YOUR INVESTMENTS

The Foggy Road

Imagine you are driving down a foggy road, and you're not exactly sure where you are. You are not even sure if you're heading in the right direction. Every mile that creeps by looks the same as the last.

You are worried that you could be lost. And you're looking for a sign.

The sign you are looking for is very specific. It tells you how many miles away you are from your destination. You want some reassurance that you are still on the right road.

Finally, you see it—the sign you've been waiting for. It tells you that you are on the right track. The anxious feeling in the pit of your stomach disappears. You keep moving forward on the road with confidence, even if the area around you is still obscured by fog. You do not need to see every detail of the landscape you're driving past. You've hit a concrete benchmark, and you feel reassured.

Progress signposts are effective ways to make sure you stay on track to reach your goals, and they aren't limited to roads. They are also a powerful tool for tracking the success of your investment strategy.

The Power of Tracking

The kind of reassurance you feel when you encounter an affirming signpost on the road is the same feeling you get when you track the results of your portfolio plan on a consistent basis. You need to make sure that you monitor not just your overall portfolio strategy, but also its individual components.

You design your portfolio to give you certain results. When you first put your plan together, you should feel confident that you have a plan in place that will take you to your goals. Especially in an investing environment impacted by constant change, your strategy should not remain static. As the market moves, you need to adjust—something I will discuss in more depth in the next chapter.

Before you can make adjustments, however, you must know what needs to be adjusted. You must identify the investment strategies that are no longer working well for you by tracking them.

You track investments by measuring results. The measurement process is important because it aligns your expectations with those of advisors you may be working with and gives you a concrete yardstick to show where you are on the path to your goals.

This chapter will show you how to track your investments within your portfolio strategy.

Measure Results

The most important thing when it comes to tracking your investments is that you do so against some kind of standard measurement. Comparative measurement will assist you in determining if you are using the right strategy.

Long-Term Goals

Long-term goals could include having enough earnings to meet costs in retirement (assisted living, healthcare, and general expenses), and leaving a significant estate for your loved ones. Whatever long-term goals you have set, your objective should be to develop a plan to successfully meet your goals.

Inflation

Combatting inflation is an important goal for most investors. Inflation is calculated using prices from a sample of representative items that is periodically collected. For example, if an investment portfolio's nominal return for a period was 10 percent, and inflation was 4 percent, the real return would be 6 percent.

Peers

Another way to evaluate your investment performance is to compare your performance with a set of peers, such as a group of mutual funds with a similar objective. For example, if your portfolio has a focus on value-oriented large-cap stocks, you might compare your portfolio with a group of large-cap value funds.

Remember, when it comes to tracking your investments against a peer group, progress is relative rather than absolute. For example, let's say you have an asset that is meant to give you a target return of 7 percent per year, and you are making 10 percent. That asset is delivering excess returns of 3 percent per year, and compared to the goal in your overall strategy, you might feel like you're doing well.

However, when you do more research in relation to the asset peer group, you may discover that everyone else is earning 12 percent returns on similar assets. That means your own investment is underperforming by 2 percent. That 2 percent may not sound like a lot, but over a long period it can add up.

Risk Comparison

Another way to use peer-group tracking is to measure comparative risk. For instance, if you and another investor both have assets that are providing 10 percent returns, then everything seems to be equal on the surface. When you dig deeper, you find that the other investor is capturing that same 10 percent return with 40 percent less risk, and is therefore much better off than you are should the market move in the other direction.

Volatility levels matter and should be a part of your comparative analysis.

Benchmark Indices

The most common way to measure your portfolio performance is to compare it against an appropriate benchmark. For example, the S&P 500 index is typically used to measure large cap US equity performance, while the MSCI EAFE index and the MSCI Emerging Market Index are used to measure ex-US-developed market equity and emerging market equity performance, respectively. Fixed-income positions are often measured against the Barclays Aggregate Bond Index. There are hundreds of indices. Select the one that best fits your portfolio strategy.

If you have a portfolio with a mix of equity and fixed-income assets (for example, 50 percent equity and 50 percent fixed income), you might compare the equity portion of the portfolio with the appropriate equity indices and the fixed-income portion with a bond index.

The way you track your investments is up to you, as long as you use the same benchmark consistently.

Due Diligence

Ronald Reagan had an old adage about the former Soviet Union: he was willing to trust, but only with verification.

Your investments should follow the same rule. You may have taken all the necessary steps to make good investments in the first place, and you may trust the people who advised you on your portfolio decisions. However, that does not mean that you can simply walk away from your investments and expect them to be effective indefinitely. You need to continually verify that everything is working as it should.

Tracking your investment portfolio may sound like a lot of work, but it does not have to be difficult. Many online resources and in-person experts can provide the assistance you need to assess your portfolio's performance.

When you track the investments you make, you can determine what needs to change in your portfolio strategy to give you optimal results. But just identifying the items that need to change isn't enough. You have to take action and make the adjustments. The next chapter will show you how to adjust your portfolio with confidence.

Chapter 7

ADJUST YOUR PORTFOLIO TO FIT THE CHANGING ENVIRONMENT

The Blue-Chip Portfolio

"It just doesn't make sense," Jack exclaimed.

It was 2009, and Jack had already been investing for twenty years and counting. He was by no means new to the world of investments, and he kept himself well informed by closely following the market via news outlets and investor conferences.

Then the strategies that had been successful for him for so long no longer seemed to work. He came to me to discuss the uncertainty in the new investing environment, looking for guidance.

"I thought for sure I had a diversified portfolio strategy with old blue-chip names that wouldn't be negatively impacted by the economy or the markets. What happened?" Jack wondered aloud, raking a hand through his hair.

"You did have a diversified blue-chip portfolio," I told him. "But the world changed, and what was once safe became perilous." Jack's portfolio had included names like AIG and Fannie Mae. These were companies that everyone considered safe until the economy crashed in 2008. Unfortunately, they weren't as safe as most people had thought.

"What happened" was not that Jack's strategy had been bad to begin with. He did indeed have a diversified blue-chip portfolio when he initially put it together.

What happened was that the economy and conditions changed dramatically, and Jack didn't adjust his strategy in time to avoid financial damage.

Flexibility in Today's Investment Environment

What is right today might not be right in the future. That is why it's so important to adjust your investment strategy on an ongoing basis to fit the environment. The world is changing rapidly—far too quickly for you to close your eyes and hope for the best for your investments.

You have to adjust your strategy consistently based on what's happening in the world. If you simply ignore your portfolio as Jack did, you might very well be disappointed with your long-term results. As the environment changes, you need to use your personal investing compass to redirect you toward the correct course you charted in the first place. Being proactive is imperative.

Industries change. Economies change. I would imagine

that thirty years ago, investing in printed newspapers was a reasonable proposition. However, with the advent of the Internet, newspapers are becoming less important in our modern world. Even if you invested in them back when it was a good idea, that asset strategy is going to need some adjusting to adapt to current conditions.

The bottom line is that you cannot afford to neglect adjusting your strategy after you create it. This chapter will outline how to make adjustments to your portfolio that will keep you moving efficiently in the direction of your goals.

A High-Level View of Your Overall Strategy

To adjust your portfolio, you need to take a step back, look at all the moving parts, and assess how those parts are impacted by today's changing environment. Then, you need to take that understanding and apply it to your strategy.

Observe the world around you to try to get a sense of how the environment is changing. Based on what is happening now, ask yourself what changes will likely occur in the economy over the next five to ten years. Will we be using gasoline-powered cars, electric cars, or hydrogen cars? Will we be driving our cars at all, or will they take us to our destinations on autopilot? How will banking and advertising change? What will happen to brick-and-mortar stores with the increased presence of online stores?

You also need to look at the world beyond the United States to anticipate how global trends will impact our economy. Are interest rates rising or falling, and what changes are being made to global interest-rate policies? How is China's economy affecting everyone else's? Will the United States become a manufacturing powerhouse once again? How will deficits impact the future of the American economy?

These and many other issues need to be assessed when you take stock of the investing environment. Every one matters, because every one affects your portfolio.

Make Changes and Rebalance

Once you have observed the larger picture, you are ready to apply that knowledge to making specific adjustments in your portfolio.

Look at every asset in your strategy, one by one. It is possible that you may still be generally on the right path, yet one or two assets simply are not performing as well as they should.

As you examine each, ask yourself: Which of these have done well, and which have not been successful based on the tracking benchmarks discussed in chapter 6? Is each asset still weighted correctly relative to the overall strategy?

If you find that an asset holds too big of a percentage in your overall portfolio strategy, carve a profit off what you've earned, and reinvest in other positions. An asset that is underweight likely means that the position hasn't done well or that everything else has done better relative to that particular asset. Ask yourself if you still believe in the thesis behind the asset, and if you do, rebalance your strategy around it accordingly.

Rebalancing your portfolio is a key part of your asset allocation strategy—and it is absolutely critical to making sure that your investments are diversified enough to meet your personal risk-return tolerance level. Do not forget to rebalance! Doing so helps you avoid over-concentrations that can significantly impact volatility levels and risk.

How Often to Make Adjustments

Investors frequently ask me how often they should adjust their portfolio strategies.

The answer really has to do with your personal philosophy and perspective. My company does not look solely at short-term horizons when we advise our clients on their portfolios. We choose to focus more on fundamentals and long-term macro-variable events, combined with short-term conditions. Still, we make adjustments when needed, even in the short term. So we look at both long- and short-term conditions when we make judgments and investment decisions.

Regardless of whether you are a short- or long-term investor, however, it makes sense to stand back at least once a quarter and see what needs to be adjusted in your portfolio strategy. Take in the big picture of how everything is unfolding, and ask yourself: Am I happy with how I am invested right now? Am I happy with the way my portfolio is structured? What changes should I make? Which assets are doing well or poorly? Has any economic or market news occurred over the last quarter that requires me to make adjustments?

Don't avoid looking at both the big and small pictures. Your portfolio requires that kind of attention.

Adjust Your Path

When NASA sends a satellite to distant galaxies, it doesn't set one course of direction and leave it at that. It adjusts that path countless times. If the path isn't updated continuously, NASA knows that the intended target may be elusive, and the goal may be missed by a wide margin.

The exact same philosophy is true for your investments.

Just because you invest with long-term goals in mind does not mean that you never need to adjust your portfolio strategy. Warren Buffet is a long-term investor, and he rebalances his portfolio every quarter. If Warren Buffet is making adjustments to his investments, the odds are good that you should do the same.

Make adjustments as often as is necessary for you. Look at your portfolio as an active organism that needs your care and attention. Do not be afraid to make changes when you need to, and don't let the fact that an asset is up or down be the sole reason for your adjustments.

Keep in mind the big picture of the ultimate future you envision for yourself. Every decision you make must be focused on moving your portfolio strategy toward the optimal risk-reward balance that you defined in chapter 3.

You cannot simply invest and forget. Someone has to pay attention. If you don't have the time to manage your investments yourself, it may be worth the cost to have an advisor working on your behalf. In the next chapter, I will show how to choose an advisor and work with that individual to get the most out of the relationship.

Chapter 8

CONSIDER WORKING WITH AN ADVISOR TO MAXIMIZE YOUR WEALTH

Ground Zero

Do you need a financial advisor? Maybe yes, maybe no. The answer depends on each person's comfort level with being involved in the management of a portfolio.

Some individuals choose to make and manage their own investments. They like watching the news and markets daily. They enjoy the research process and have the time required to be their own portfolio managers. The lessons in this book are not foreign to them; they are proactive and consistently adjust, reallocate, and assess their portfolios. They have not only the time but also the interest and skill to make decisions on their asset strategies.

If this sounds like you, you may not need an advisor.

However, working with an advisor is a more reasonable option for many investors. They have neither the time nor inclination to be involved in the details of their strategies.

They are starting from ground zero, and they need help.

What to Expect from an Advisor

Don't select just anyone to be your advisor. The person you choose needs to meet your high expectations, and you should never settle for "good enough." Here's what the right advisor should be expected to do for you.

An advisor should be like a consultant who understands your financial goals and your views on money and financial matters. He or she walks the path with you. When you feel confused or overwhelmed with the task of figuring out your investment strategy and your overall financial plan, your advisor should provide clarity.

Experienced advisors can tell you what challenges stand in the way of you achieving your goals, and how those issues need to be addressed. You should be able to have clear discussions with your advisor about your return expectations based on the amount of risk you are willing to take within your portfolio strategy. The right advisor can tell you the best mix of assets for your portfolio and share with you the mistakes to avoid.

The right advisor can help you think through the things that you know are important, but do not have the time or knowledge to handle yourself. He or she can also help you remain calm during market storms and reassure you that your portfolio is invested correctly under the current conditions.

Many people underestimate the importance of long-term financial planning. An advisor that focuses on your long-term wealth accumulation should be prepared to provide thoughtful, expert planning help.

Imagine for a moment that you are planning your next vacation. How much time would you take to figure out the best flight, the right seat on the plane, the nicest hotel, and so forth? For most people, the amount of time spent doing that exceeds the time they have ever spent putting together a retirement plan that will set the framework for an investment strategy.

That paradigm needs to change, and a good advisor can help you develop an appropriate plan to achieve your goals. The next logical question then becomes, how do you choose and work with a quality advisor?

The Right Qualifications

There is no law that says an individual must meet certain standards to call him or herself a financial advisor. Anyone, with virtually no experience, can get a business card that says "financial planning" on it and hand it to you on no greater authority than that. So how can you tell a good advisor from the rest?

The first thing to look at when choosing a quality advisor is qualifications. These qualifications should demonstrate that the individual has done the necessary preparation to be a professional in good standing. A good standard to go by is whether the person has completed the prestigious Certified Financial Planning (CFP®) designation provided by the Certified Financial Planner Board of Standards. Check regulatory agencies for complaints or compliance issues. Both the Securities and Exchange Commission and FINRA have an online repository that outlines any past issues.

Assess the educational background of the advisor. While education is not a guarantee of quality, it does show the commitment of the advisor to the profession. Remember, not all great advisors have related background in the advisory field, so feel free to ask what other educational qualifications they might have. A committed advisor seeks to improve his or her skillset through ongoing training and education.

The ideal advisor should also have considerable experience. He or she should have been through a rigorous process of understanding how investments work, tax planning, estate planning, retirement analysis, college-funding strategies, and other financial planning issues. An advisor who can provide financial planning guidance combined with an explanation of investment alternatives is the type of professional from whom you can benefit most as you create your overall strategy.

The right advisor should also understand investment fluctuation, risk return issues, asset allocation, and how to structure portfolios that meet your requirements with as little risk as possible. He or she should understand markets and economies.

A quality advisor should furthermore be skilled in communication and should always listen carefully to what you are trying to accomplish. You want someone whom you are comfortable communicating with, and who can explain complicated issues in a clear manner.

Finally, although you can certainly have a successful relationship with a sole financial advisor, you may want to consider finding someone who is part of an established team of seasoned professionals. Teams of advisors bring something to the table that individual advisors lack: greater experience across a broad range of areas. Collaborative environments can offer the most thorough offering of resources to guide your investments.

It can make sense to work with a firm that has a group of Certified Financial Planners on your side. A team of professionals covering complex financial topics together may be able to bring the best practices of the entire group to you and your situation.

When searching for a quality advisor or team of advisors, never hesitate to ask for references and experience. Quality advisors are proud of their professional dedication and will be delighted to provide you with their qualifications and a list of references.

Work with Your Advisor

Once you've identified and signed on with an advisor who you believe is a good fit for you, how do you get the most out of your working relationship?

First, always keep in mind that your advisor works for you. There is no reason to be intimidated or afraid to ask questions. You need to be comfortable asking questions at any time. An advisor should always be willing to carefully explain his or her thinking while constructing a portfolio strategy for you.

With this in mind, the relationship between you and your advisor should be one of collaborative partnership and choices. Some advisors take the approach of, "I alone know what is best." While you can certainly operate with this type of advisor perspective, it may be better to engage with your advisor as a partner. This gives you input on decisions related to your money and can give you a clearer understanding of the potential rewards and consequences of those decisions.

Your advisor should be open to adjusting strategies based on your personal comfort level, and you should never settle for a one-size-fits-all recommendation. Defensiveness should be the last thing you encounter when discussing your investment strategy and results with your advisor.

Always remember that advisors are paid to provide information and expertise, as well as to coach you in the investing process. Don't settle for a strained relationship.

The Power of Chemistry

One final key to remember when selecting an advisor is this: do not underestimate the power of chemistry.

Qualifications and experience are great. However, in the end, you are dealing with more than cold statistics. Your advisor is someone who knows the intimate details of your financial situation and what your life goals are. You should therefore work with someone who feels like the right fit for you.

When you choose your advisor, you are forming a partnership that will last for years. Do not take this financial-planning and investment marriage lightly. It is an important relationship designed to move you toward long-term success and the only retirement you will have in your lifetime.

At this stage in the process, your personal investor's compass has guided you to a portfolio strategy that is designed for your goals. The next chapter will cover the best part of investing: enjoying your money.

Chapter 9

ENJOY YOUR MONEY

Go Ahead, Buy the Curtains

"Hi Michael. I just have a quick question for you. I'm thinking of buying new drapes for my house. It will probably cost $5,000. I just want to make sure there's enough money in my investment strategy to redecorate my windows."

Not long after I got that call, a different client rang me up with a similar question. He wanted to know if he could get rid of his twenty-year-old car and buy a new one—maybe one of those new hybrid vehicles he'd been hearing so much about.

Both of these sound like reasonable questions on the surface. But underneath, they had something in common that would seem surprising to most outside observers.

In each case, the person asking the question had several million dollars in his or her investment portfolio. Both had accumulated more net worth than they had ever imagined possible.

Yet despite the assets they had attained, both individuals also had a tangible fear of poverty. They had been raised by Depression-era family members, and between that and personal circumstances earlier in their lives, they often worried about money and whether they would one day end up homeless and broke.

They were afraid to enjoy their money.

The Great Irony of Investing

Investors who have adequate money are the ones who have been fiscally responsible and saved for retirement their whole lives. These individuals have lived without new cars and other new things, because they wanted to have a wonderful retirement instead.

The great irony is that once they arrive at retirement, their old habits make it difficult for them to spend the money they have saved. What often ends up happening is that these investors end up having excess amounts of money when they pass away—money that they could have used to enjoy their lives in retirement.

Investing is about more than surviving in retirement. The whole reason for investing in the first place is to give you the ability to live life on your terms. You may discipline yourself for years as you are accumulating wealth, but in the end the old adage is true that "you can't take it with you." Enjoying your money is the reward you claim in exchange for the sacrifices you have made.

Attitudes and values toward money are not easily changed. The Depression scarred many people, and they passed down to their children the fear of not knowing where the next meal was coming from. That event is just one example of any number of things that inspire a deep fear of not having enough in later years.

I understand that feeling. I worked through college at grocery stores and restaurants. The only way I made it through school was with the assistance of grants and loans. I drove old cars with old tires, and I still remember the days of filling my gas tank with one dollar of gas. Even today, I still hesitate to buy anything that is not on sale. Old habits die hard.

When the facts demonstrate that you have nothing to fear, however, it's important to recognize that you can be financially prudent and still enjoy your money at the same time.

Plan to Enjoy

Your plan for your money should include enjoyment. That is the power of a financial plan. It can tell you on a real-time basis where you stand relative to your long-term financial objectives. It can reassure you that there are enough resources to enjoy your retirement, rather than merely cover minimum living costs. In this way, the right plan can bring you freedom.

For example, many people say they want to travel in retirement. Wouldn't it be wonderful to have a special fund in your portfolio strategy dedicated specifically to that goal? This means that within the strategy itself, a certain amount of income flows to you for traveling, and you can spend it any time you want on travel activity. Or perhaps instead you like baseball, and you want to follow your favorite team around the country. Or maybe you want to take a cruise to a new part of the world every quarter.

The goal itself can be anything. What matters is making sure that your strategy is set up not only to cover your standard of living expenses, but also to give you the opportunity to enjoy your money.

What Really Matters

In these chapters, I have outlined a simple way for you to think about your portfolio and a process that can help you consider what actions to take. I have not gone into the detailed specifics of how to make different investments or suggested a particular strategy that is right for you. I've avoided doing those things on purpose, because where this book is concerned, they aren't what really matters.

What really matters is you.

Your goals are what matter. Living life as you want to live it is what matters. Your money and especially your future are what matter. That is the real goal of successful investing. Your investment strategy has to be designed specifically for you.

You now have the foundation that will allow you to invest for growth, freedom, and peace of mind in a changing environment. You know how to identify your value system and apply it to your decisions. You know how to find the people who will advise you on the best decisions to make, taking into account your views on money and long-term goals.

You have worked a lifetime to get to the point where you can have comfort and live on your terms. When you define your individual philosophy and use it to create a personalized structure for investing, your money will help you live the life you've imagined.

When the day is done, remember to enjoy the fruits of your hard work and live the life you have been working toward. Whatever course you chart from here, I sincerely wish you the best of success as you travel your own unique financial path.

Enjoy your money.

ABOUT THE AUTHOR

Michael Yoshikami, Ph.D., CFP®, is CEO and Founder of Destination Wealth Management and Chairman of DWM's Portfolio Strategy Committee. Founded in 1986, Destination is a San Francisco Bay Area-based independent firm that provides fee-based wealth management services to institutional and individual investors. Michael was named by Barron's[1] as one of the "Top 100 Independent Financial Advisors", seven years in a row (2009 – 2015).

Michael has over thirty years experience in the investment management and financial planning field. As Chairman of the Portfolio Strategy Committee, he oversees the macro tactical asset allocation weightings for client portfolios and develops the economic viewpoints that guide portfolio strategy.

Michael provides investment commentary for CNBC U.S., CNBC Europe and CNBC Asia. He also

1 Barron's "Top 100 Independent Advisors" is based on the volume of assets under management, revenues the advisor generate for their firm and the quality of their practices. The scoring system assigns a top score of 100 and rates the rest by comparing them to the winner. The Barron's award is not indicative of Destination Wealth Management future performance.

provides commentary to Reuters, CBS Radio, Dow Jones, the Wall Street Journal, and other international publications. Michael also publishes a weekly investment focused newsletter. He holds a Ph.D. in education, and has earned the Certified Financial Planner (CFP®) designation.

More information about the firm and Michael Yoshikami can be found at www.destinationwm.com.

destination
WEALTH MANAGEMENT

Founded in 1986, Destination Wealth Management is an independent wealth management firm offering investment management services and advice to individuals and institutional investors.

PROACTIVE INVESTMENT STRATEGY

The current economic and market environment suggests that a new investment approach is necessary. Destination Wealth Management has the capability and insight to help investors in today's uncertain world. Our investment team designs portfolio strategies based on clients' goals while integrating tactical adjustments given current economic and market dynamics. Considerations include:

- Risk assessment

- Taxation analysis for portfolio adjustments

- Economic and market tactical tilts

- Mapping of portfolio strategy to stated planning goals

PLANNING SERVICES

Our team of advisors have years of experience in analyzing wealth management issues and hold industry credentials such as the Certified Financial Planner (CFP®). Financial planning advice and services are provided to our clients at no additional cost and include the following:

- Retirement projections

- Income planning

- Education funding

- Tax and estate planning

- Stock options and concentrated positions

- Risk management and insurance review

HERE TO HELP

For more information call us at 855.DWM.PLAN

www.destinationwm.com

info@destinationwm.com

@DestinationWM

facebook.com/destinationwm

linkedin.com/company/destinationwealth-management